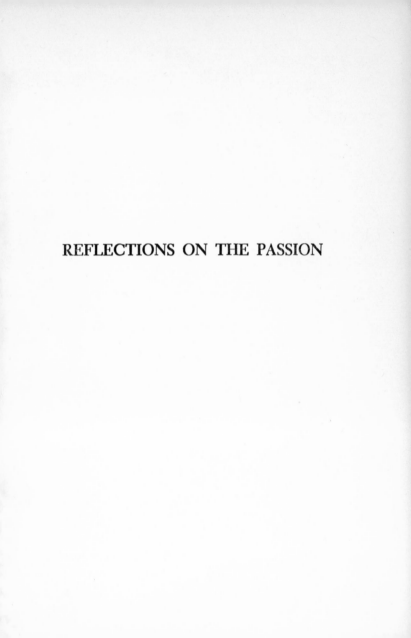

REFLECTIONS ON THE PASSION

REFLECTIONS
on the PASSION

BY CHARLES HUGO DOYLE

THE BRUCE PUBLISHING COMPANY
MILWAUKEE

NIHIL OBSTAT:

  JOANNES A. SCHULIEN, S.T.D.
  Censor librorum

IMPRIMATUR:

  ✠ ALBERTUS G. MEYER
  Archiepiscopus Milwauchiensis

  October 25, 1956

Rosary College Dewey Classification Number: 232.96

Library of Congress Catalog Card Number: 57–6320

To

His Excellency

JOHN HUGH MacDONALD, D.D.

Archbishop of Edmonton, Alberta, Canada,

as a filial tribute

on the occasion of his

GOLDEN JUBILEE

CONTENTS

8 CONTENTS

REFLECTIONS ON THE PASSION

LOVE moves and governs all things. Tell me what you love, and I shall tell you what you are. If your love is for the world, you are its slave. If your love is for Jesus Christ, you are free; you are becoming conformed to His image; your conversation, that is your life and conduct even here below, are continually in heaven.

Jesus Christ is alone worthy of your whole heart. But you cannot love Him if you do not know Him. It is not enough to know that "God so loved the world as to give His only-begotten Son," that "He emptied Himself out," and that "He laid down His life for His flock." We must know the *details* of His sufferings, if we would know the excess of His love.

This little volume — REFLECTIONS ON THE PASSION — was written for just this purpose. It should provide the laity with short, pointed considerations for quiet prayer, the religious, with ready material for personal and profitable meditation, and the clergy, with suitable matter for before-Mass reading to the faithful or for sermon seeds for Lenten courses.

11

Ash Wednesday

IT IS related that King Louis XIV of France, shortly after his ascent to the throne, stood at an open window in his palace and silently admired the simple beauty of the Church of St. Denis, standing some distance away. A servant ventured to remark that all the king's ancestors lay buried in that church and that, doubtless, it would also be His Majesty's last resting place. The very next day the king ordered another palace built so that the Church of St. Denis would be hidden from his view.

It is a weakness in our nature to try to soften the full force of the disconcerting truth that we all must die. We do our best to keep from dwelling too much on this fact lest its morbidity depress us. Expensive caskets with their silk linings, the flowers, the green imitation grass thrown over the newly turned soil in the cemetery, are all designed to pamper our squeamishness about death.

Holy Mother the Church is much more realistic. She has her priests bless ashes, and then place some of these ashes on the foreheads of her children, saying at the same time, "Remember, man, thou art but dust, and into dust thou shalt return."

Sin and death go together. Because Adam and Eve sinned in the Garden of Eden, they had to submit to this dreadful penalty, and in like manner, all their descendants. To remind us of this grim fact, the Church places ashes on the foreheads of her children on each Ash Wednesday, saying, "Remember, man, thou art but dust, and into dust thou shalt return."

There is still another death which the Church would remind us of today — the death of our vices and concupiscences through mortification and penance. The word *mortification* comes from two Latin words meaning "To make death"; and so in asking us to mortify ourselves during Lent, the Church begs us to deaden our appetites and passions by discipline so that we might live supernatural lives.

The imposition of ashes, then, is not only symbolic of death, but of penance and mortification too. Since there would be no death if there had not been sin, so there can be no supernatural life without mortification and penance. The ashes on our foreheads should so remind us, since holy men like Job and David associated ashes with penance, and the Church has been doing the same thing for almost 2000 years.

So you see, life, death, mortification, and penance are all brought to our minds by the simple but deeply meaningful ceremony of the imposition of the blessed ashes. Could a more effective way be found to signify the beginning of the penitential season of Lent? The external application of the ashes to our foreheads will be useless and meaningless unless and until we resolve in our hearts to use the forty days ahead to do penance in reparation for our past failures and practice mortification to condition our souls and bodies for the struggles ahead.

Spend some time today in considering the fact that you will sooner or later die and that everyone and everything you hold near and dear to you must be left behind. "To fear death *before* it comes," says St. Gregory, "is to conquer it *when* it comes."

Say often this prayer of David: "O Lord, make me know my end, and what is the number of my days that I may know what is wanting in me" (Ps. 38:5).

Thursday After Quinquagesima Sunday

TRUE devotion in its highest meaning includes love for, and imitation of, the person to whom we are devoted, and Holy Mother the Church presents for our prayerful devotion during Lent the Sacred Passion of our Lord Jesus Christ, with the fervent hope that we shall be aroused to imitate Him.

"We should," writes Father Degnam, S.J., "go through the different circumstances of the Passion, and compare them with the occasions of sufferings we meet with in life. They are drops of the chalice which our Lord asks us to drink with Him. His sufferings of the scourging, our physical pain; He is treated as a fool by Herod; He was rejected for Barabbas; are we not sometimes rejected for another — set aside for some one who is certainly more worthy than ourselves? Is not the gall they gave Him to drink like the bitterness we receive when we are longing for consolation? As we look at the dead Body of our Lord hanging on the Cross, we see that His Passion was one long act of submission."

Gratitude should fill our hearts at the thought of God's goodness to us in giving us His own adorable Son as a Model to imitate, so that we have only to look at Him to know what we have to do. Hear Christ Himself say: "I have given you an example, that as I have done to you, so you also should do" (Jn. 13:15). Christ is the only way we must follow, especially in the practice of virtue, and it was during the Passion that His practice of the virtues was strikingly sublime and heroic. In the most trying circumstances our Lord gave us during the Passion examples of those virtues we somehow seem to lack — meekness, mercy, charity, silence, patience, abandonment, and obedience to His Father's will — even unto death.

Well did St. Bonaventure say: "He who desires to go on advancing from virtue to virtue, from grace to grace, should constantly meditate on the Passion of Jesus Christ."

Daily, during the holy season of Lent, let us consider together some detail of the Sacred Passion and death of our Saviour, beginning with the agony in the Garden. Endeavor to seize upon one thought and keep turning it over in your mind during the day. Try to see the *virtue* practiced by the Master and resolve to imitate that virtue. Strive to find some *lesson* in each of these daily considerations and resolve to put it into practice during the day. In your examination of conscience at night, examine yourself on how you kept the resolution taken that morning. Little good will result from the study of the Passion unless such a study results in our imitation of Christ. "O foolish Galatians!" cried out St. Paul, "who has bewitched you [that you should not obey the truth], before whose eyes Jesus Christ has been depicted crucified?" (Gal. 3:1.)

After the Last Supper, Christ gathered the Apostles around Him and they set out together for Gethesemani, the Garden of Agony. The name "Gethsemani" is interesting in that it means "oilpress"; in other words, it was a place where the fresh olives were pressed and the oil extracted. What a symbolic spot chosen by the Sacred Redeemer of Mankind for the initial and awful beginning of the Passion! Here He was to take upon Himself the sins of the world and be so crushed under their terrible weight that His precious blood flowed from every pore of His body.

With reverence, then, and with contrite hearts let us begin our contemplation of the Passion of our Lord in the Garden of Gethsemani and pray that your heart and soul will be inflamed with love and aroused to imitate all the virtues practiced by the Saviour in His Passion.

Decide now on one positive act of mortification to be practiced this very day, recalling these words of the *Imitation of Christ:* "The more thou dost violence to thyself, the greater thy progress will be."

Tomorrow we shall see our Lord separating Peter, James, and John from the other Apostles and taking them with Him into the midst of the Garden. Thus we shall begin our study of the Passion.

Friday After Quinquagesima Sunday

OUR BLESSED LORD had designedly planned that Peter, James, and John should be afforded but a glimpse of His divinity when it burst forth on the occasion of His Transfiguration. Now in the Garden of Olives these same Apostles would see their Lord and their God bent and crushed under the weight of sin. The thought of the Transfiguration would have to strengthen them in this hour of disillusionment.

The Apostles had always known our Lord to be composed in the face of attack or crisis. For instance, when the elements of nature tossed their fishing boats until they, hardened fishermen though they were, quaked with fear, Christ was calm and unafraid; but in the Garden of Gethsemani they were to see this same Christ prostrate on the ground, bathed in a sweat of blood. That which made up the very essence of the anguish of Gethesmani was the fact that Christ, at that moment, took upon Himself the sins of the world — past, present, and future.

But why had Christ invited the Apostles to accompany Him to the Garden of Olives? Well, as He entered the darkness, He may have craved human companionship. It was not that the Apostles could do anything for Him, but that their very presence would support Him. Too, He wanted to teach them some important lessons.

The first lesson was this, that when one is oppressed, discouraged, heartbroken, and forsaken, he should pray. That is what our Lord did. He was afraid. He was overwhelmed by the sins of mankind, His Apostles, His closest friends, fell asleep — yet He prayed. Always remember what our Lord told His weak Apostles when He awakened them the first time: "Watch and pray, that you may not enter into temptation. The spirit indeed is willing, but the flesh is weak" (Mt. 26:41).

The second lesson is equally apparent. While Christ's closest friends were asleep as He went through the initial phases of the Passion, His enemies were very much awake. At that very moment Judas was briefing the soldiers on where to find Christ and how to apprehend Him. The soldiers were getting themselves ready to arrest the Son of God.

So it has always been, and always will be — the enemies of your soul and mine, the enemies of Christ and His Church never sleep. They are always more vigilant, more energetic, more active than we are.

Resolve today to make a visit to the Blessed Sacrament and let the picture of Christ in the Garden of Olives come to your mind. Approach your prostrate King — promise Him to do some positive penance for the sins you have committed. Ask Him to teach you this important lesson — that when doubts, trials, sorrows, and temptations assail you, you, following His example, will pray, pray, pray.

 ## Saturday After Quinquagesima Sunday

OUR LORD had suffered a terrible ordeal in His initial phase of trial in the Garden of Olives. He had, some thirty-three years earlier, taken on the burden of human nature. Now in this fateful garden, Christ took on the awful burden of man's sins, and He rightfully looked to His closest friends to share His burden in return, if only by compassion. They failed Him. They slept. Oh how the words of the prophet were fulfilled: "I looked for one that would grieve together with me, and there was none; for one that would comfort me, and I found none" (Ps. 68:21).

Note that our Lord goes back a second time to pray. This time He is even more alone than before. He prays to

His Father, and His heavenly Father turns a deaf ear to His petition. His disciples are sleeping again, and yet He prays on alone. He is now in a state of supreme desolation and yet He prays. He is in a state of complete dereliction but He prays on. Learn from this lesson to pray even under the most adverse circumstances.

Consider the fact that Christ persevered in His prayer. Already He had prayed to His Father saying: "Father, if it is possible, let this cup pass away from me" (Mt. 26:39). That prayer was unanswered.

The second prayer of our Lord was a repetition of the first, for He said: "My Father, if this cup cannot pass away unless I drink it, thy will be done" (Mt. 26:42).

The third prayer was couched in the same words — a prayer more fervent, more earnest than any uttered by any man who ever lived on this earth — yet His Father, it seemed, did not listen to His petition. Christ did not grow impatient, He calmly and resignedly adds: "Not my will but thine be done" (Lk. 22:42).

What a great lesson in this for all of us! If the Son of God must plead three times for the fulfillment of His prayer, and does so without a trace of bitterness, why are we so depressed when our prayers are not immediately answered? St. Monica prayed for eighteen years for her son Augustine's conversion, but how richly her perseverance was rewarded. "We wait a whole year," says St. Francis de Sales, "before the seed we sow in the ground bears fruit; and are we more impatient in regard to the fruits of our prayers?"

There is great consolation for all of us in the refusal of the Father to hear the petition of His adorable son. God the Father refused the most perfect, the most precious prayer ever uttered on this earth — but He did so to prove His love for sinful man. For the sake of sinful man He will not answer the prayer of His own Son, because, had God acted otherwise, we would all have been lost. See the reason behind God's refusal to answer our prayers — He always has the greater good in view:

From now on, never complain if your prayers are unanswered. Just keep right on praying. Say your rosary today for the great grace of perseverance.

 ## Monday After the First Sunday in Lent

OUR consideration of the triple prayer of our Blessed Lord in the Garden of Olives should have convinced us of the merit and necessity of continued prayer when we are afraid, downcast, depressed, tempted, or forsaken.

There were numerous other occasions when Christ addressed petitions to His eternal Father and the response was immediate. The raising of Lazarus is a case in point. In the Garden of Olives, however, the Master prayed three times and His prayer was unanswered. We have seen that had God the Father answered Christ's prayer and "let the cup pass away" from Him, the world might not yet be redeemed. When God does not answer prayer it is for a greater good.

In the Old Testament we read that the prophet Elias, when he asked God to confound the pagan prophets of Baal by a miracle, hardly had spoken his prayer when a miraculous fire came down from heaven and consumed a holocaust set on the altar, and even burned water in the trench. When the same prophet Elias prayed for rain for God's people, he had to repeat his prayer not once, twice, or three times, but seven times (3 Kings 18:44).

When God refuses to answer prayer it is for a greater good. When He delays the answer it is to put the endurance of the suppliant to a severe test.

The Jews in Bethulia prayed all night, desiring the help of the God of Israel when Holofernes besieged their city, but the more they prayed, the more desperate the situation appeared. Yet they persevered, and God sent them a deliverer in Judith.

Another important lesson which we can learn from our Lord's prayer in Gethsemani is this, that all our petitions to God should close in acquiescence to the divine will. Hear our Lord say in the depths of His agony — "Not my will but thine be done" (Lk. 22:42).

It is right for us to plead earnestly for what we want — earnestly, perseveringly, but never insubmissively. We should recognize that God will not give us what will do more harm than good. Many of us have lived long enough to thank God that He did not give us what we asked in prayer in every instance.

The best thing possible for us is always what God wills for us. Sometimes it may be pain, worldly loss, or some bereavement; yet His will is always love, and in simple acquiescence to God's will, we shall always find our highest good. No prayer, therefore, is pleasing to God which does not end with the refrain of Gethsemani: "Not my will but Thine be done."

This is the way to peace, for as we yield with love and joy, and merge our will with God's, His peace will flow like a river into our souls.

Resolve that each time today you hear a clock strike the hour, you will say reverently, "Not my will but Thine be done."

Tuesday After the First Sunday in Lent

CHRIST prayed three times in the Garden of Olives. After each prayer was finished, and the words of those three prayers, by the way, were nearly identical, the Master went back to His Apostles, and in each instance He found them asleep.

Between the first and second sessions of prayer, our Lord uttered a powerful warning, for He said to the drowsy disciples: "Watch and pray, that you may not enter into temptation. The spirit is willing, but the flesh is weak" (Mt. 26:41).

"Watch and pray, that you may not enter into temptation" is a powerful warning that no man should disregard. In wartime it is not unusual to find a soldier court-martialed and summarily executed for falling asleep at his post. Life is a constant warfare against the legions of hell, and we must be ever watchful against sudden attacks from the enemy. But to watch alone is not enough. A sentinel posted on the walls, when he perceives the enemy gathering for an attack, would be foolhardy indeed, to presume to engage the enemy singlehanded. The wise soldier would send word to his commanding officer of the enemy's approach. Watchfulness lies in observing the imminent approach of the enemy and prayer is the telling of it to God. Watchfulness without prayer is presumption, and prayer without watchfulness is a mockery.

The great Abbot John remarked that a man who is asleep at the foot of a tree and sees a wild animal coming toward him to devour him, will most certainly climb up into the tree to save himself. "So we," says the Abbot, "when we perceive ourselves beset with temptations, ought to climb up to heaven and by the help of prayer, retire safely into the bosom of God."

The saints have taught that short prayers are most effective in time of temptation. St. Athanasius, for instance, taught that the opening phrase of the sixty-seventh psalm produced miraculous effects for those who used it in time of temptation. Here are the words: "Let God arise, and let His enemies be scattered, and let those that hate Him fly before His face."

Note well, that our Lord did not tell His disciples to pray to be *relieved* of temptations altogether, but rather, that they "enter not into temptation." God tempts no man, but He permits us to be tempted so to prove ourselves. "Blessed is the man who endures temptation; for when he has been tried, he will receive the crown of life" (James 1:12). St. Bernard, explaining these inspired words of St. James, says: "it is necessary that temptations should happen, for who shall be crowned but he that shall lawfully have fought, and how shall a man fight, if there be none to attack him?"

Be undeceived — position, piety, or experience will not spare you temptations. Adam fell when he was in the state of grace and Peter fell soon after his first Holy Communion.

Resolve today to make use of the holy names of Jesus, Mary, and Joseph in the very outset of any temptation. Try to commit the first sentence of Psalm 67 to heart, and promise yourself to make use of it as soon as you discern the approach of any temptation.

 ## Wednesday After the First Sunday in Lent

AS CHRIST ended His third prayer in the Garden of Gethsemani, He lay prostrate on the ground horribly shaken by the whole ordeal. The one thing He prayed for was not granted Him, but Holy Scripture relates that, "there appeared to him an angel from heaven to strengthen him" (Lk. 22:43).

It was an angel from heaven who announced to His mother Mary that she had been chosen to fulfill a creature's greatest service to her God. When men refused the Son of God recognition on this earth, angels filled the skies to announce Him and sing His glories. When cruel men sought His life in infancy, an angel directed the Holy Family to the safety of Egypt. When He was tempted in the desert: "Behold angels came and ministered to him" (Mt. 4:11). Little wonder then that when He was in agony in the Garden of Olives an angel should succor Him.

It is well to note that Christ's prayer was not answered

in the way He had desired. He had prayed the first time
that the chalice might pass from Him. It did not pass but
His strength was increased. He prayed the second time for
relief from His burden, but while the burden was increased,
His strength was augmented to match it. Christ prayed
the third time, saying the selfsame words He had spoken
on the two previous occasions. His agony did not cease but
He found the courage "to pray the more earnestly" (Lk.
22:43). Learn from this that when God seems most deaf
to our pleadings in prayer, He may prefer to make heroes
of us. Be assured that in time of temptation, and trial,
God's angels will ever be at our side to comfort, encourage,
and succor us.

Seize this occasion to bolster your devotion to the
angels, and in a special way, to St. Michael. St. Alphonsus
Liguori says: "Devotion to St. Michael is a sign of predes-
tination." In the year 1751, St. Michael appeared to an
illustrious servant of God, Antonia d'Astonae, a Carmelite
in Portugal. He expressed the wish that she should publish
for his honor nine salutations corresponding to the nine
choirs of angels. It was to consist in the recitation of a
Pater and three *Aves* in honor of each of the angelic hier-
archies, then four *Paters*, the first in his honor, the second
in honor of St. Gabriel, the third for St. Raphael, and the
last for the Guardian Angel. As a reward the glorious prince
of the celestial court promised:

"Whoever would practice this devotion in his honor
would have, when approaching the Holy Table, an escort
of nine angels chosen from each one of the nine choirs." In
addition, for the daily recital of these nine salutations he
promised his "continual assistance and that of all the holy

angels during life, and after death deliverance from purgatory for themselves and their relations."

In time of temptation call upon the holy angels and archangels to defend and protect you. Never let a day go by without a special petition to the heavenly choirs — especially your guardian angel.

 ## Thursday After the First Sunday in Lent

IN THE Transfiguration on Mount Thabor, our Blessed Lord's body was bathed in light and His divinity burst through the frail human bonds that were united to it. In the Garden of Gethsemani, the human body of the Son of God was bathed in a bloody sweat that rushed from every pore. Once the angel had strengthened our Lord, the transformation was amazing. From that moment on to the end of the Passion, we shall never see Him falter, for even one moment. He had strength for Himself and strength for all those who came to Him or crossed His path.

The moment the third prayer was ended, Holy Scripture notes that Christ went to His disciples and said: "Sleep on now, and take your rest! It is enough; the hour has come" (Mk. 14:41). The time for watching was past. Christ had passed through His agony, and on His adorable face was the radiance of peace and the fire of zeal. No longer did He need the help or the sympathy which in vain He had sought in the darkness. He looked toward the city gate, and there was the traitor coming. There was

neither need nor use now for the disciples' waking and
watching, and they might as well sleep on. The lesson is
plain. Whatever we do for our friends, we must do when
they are in need of our help. If one is sick, the time to
show sympathy is while the sickness continues. If we allow
him to pass through his illness without showing him any
attention, there is little use, when he is well again, for
us to offer kindness.

When one of our friends is passing through some sore
struggle with temptation, then is the time for us to come
close to him and put the strength of our love under his
weakness. Of what use is our help when the battle has been
fought through to the end and won without us? Or suppose
the friend was not victorious; that he failed — failed because
no one came to help him, is there any use in our hurrying
up to him then to offer assistance?

It was Ruskin who once wrote these words: "Such help
as we can give to each other in this world is a debt we owe
to each other; and the man who perceives a superiority or a
capacity in a subordinate, and neither confesses nor assists
it, is not merely the withholder of kindness, but the com-
mitter of evil."

If we are inclined to criticize the weakness of the
Apostles in sleeping rather than comforting their Lord and
their God in His hour of agony, do we not do a similar
deed when we withhold help and consolation from our
neighbor. "As long as you did not do it for one of these
least ones, you did not do it for me" (Mt. 25:44). Let
us always see Christ in our neighbor and this very day make
a real effort to be a support, comfort, and defense of someone who needs our help — spiritual or temporal. Never let

the sun set any day without having done one charitable act for a neighbor. Remember always these words of Holy Scripture: "that one's neighbor should be loved as oneself is a greater thing than all holocausts and sacrifices" (Mk. 12:33).

 Friday After the First Sunday in Lent

THE ordeal of Gethsemani now over, our Blessed Lord walks with a sort of triumph toward His sleeping Apostles. Three times He had counseled them to pray, three times He had asked them to watch with Him and three times the Apostles had failed Him.

Just anger had surged through Christ when He took a rope and drove the money-changers from the temple, because they had dishonored His Father's house. His closest friends who, a few short hours earlier, had received their first Holy Communion, had failed Him, and failed Him badly in His hour of need — surely He would have been justified had He upbraided them. But no. The gentle Christ walked over to where they took their rest, and simply said: "Rise, let us go" (Mk. 14:42). Oh, the hope that springs up from those words!

The disciples had failed sadly in one great duty — they had slept when the Master wanted them to watch with Him. They slept at their post. He had just told them that they might as well sleep on, so far as that service was concerned, for the time to render it was gone forever. Yet there were other duties before them, and Jesus calls them to arise and meet these. Because they had failed in one hour's responsibility they must not sink down in despair. They must arouse themselves to meet the responsibilities that lay ahead of them.

What a consoling lesson for all of us. Because we have failed in one duty, or many duties, we must not give up in despair. Because a young man or woman has wasted youth, he or she must not therefore lose heart and think all is lost. There are other opportunities just ahead. The loss of youth is irreparable. The golden years can never be recalled — the innocence, the beauty, the power may have slipped through our fingers — but why should we squander all because we have squandered some? Because the morning has been thrown away, why should all the day be lost?

The lesson Christ taught at the end of His agony in Gethsemani is for all who have failed in any way. Christ ever calls to hope. He bids us rise again from the worst defeats. With Christ there is always margin enough to start again and to build a noble life. Right down to the doorway of death there is time. Paul persecuted the Church, but died for it. The door of opportunity opened to the penitent thief on the cross in his dying hour. So it is always. In this world, blessed by divine love and grace, there is never need to despair. The call after every defeat or failure still is, and always will be, "Rise, let us go."

Strive every day to make acts of faith, hope, and charity. Today let us beg for an increase of the virtue of hope.

Saturday After the First Sunday in Lent

WHEN our Lord was saying to His Apostles: "Rise, let us go," He added these painful words: "He who will betray me is at hand" (Mk. 14:42). St. John gives us a few more details for he writes: "Now Judas, who betrayed him, also knew the place, since Jesus had often met there together with his disciples. Judas, then, taking the cohort, and the attendants from the chief priests and Pharisees, came there with lanterns, and torches, and weapons" (Jn. 18:2–4).

The story of Judas is perhaps the saddest in all of the Bible. The Evangelists seem fascinated with that name Judas and when they have occasion to pen it, they call him either "Judas, one of the twelve" or "the traitor" or as we have just seen St. John do, in the quote above, "Judas, who betrayed Him." The thought that one of their number could stoop to such a villainous act inflicts them with a personal shame.

Any way you look at it, the story of the betrayal shows new evil each time you read it. Going out from the supper table, Judas had hastened to the priests and was quickly on his way with the band of soldiers. He probably hurried back to the upper room, where he had left Jesus: not finding Him there, he knew well where the Master had gone, and hastened to the sacred place of prayer — Gethsemani — where Jesus had so often retired for prayer.

Then the manner in which he let the officers know which of the company was Jesus shows the deepest blackness of all. Under the guise of close friendship — Judas kissed Christ — with feigned warmth and affection.

It would be salutary for each of us to remember always how the treason in the heart of Judas grew. In the beginning, it was greed for money, then followed theft and falseness of life, ending, at last, in the blackest crime this world has ever seen. The fact that such a fall as that of Judas began with small infidelities which grew and grew into a heinous crime, should teach us the danger of committing venial sins. The Holy Ghost warns us that "he that contemneth little things, shall fall by little and little" (Eccles: 19:1).

A picture in the royal gallery of Brussels represents Judas wandering about in the night after the betrayal. He comes by chance upon the workmen who have been making the cross upon which Christ shall be crucified the next day. A fire nearby throws its full light on the faces of the workmen, who are sleeping peacefully, while resting from their labors. Judas' face is somewhat in the shade, but it is wonderfully expressive of awful remorse and agony as he catches sight of the cross and the tools used to make it — the cross which his treachery had made possible. Judas did not fall into one great sin, he began with lesser sins, and they paved the way to his great disaster.

St. John Chrysostom said this of venial sins: "I maintain that small sins require to be avoided with more care than the more grievous ones, for the grievous ones of their very nature stir up our attention against them; whereas, the lesser sins, from the fact of their being insignificant in comparison, are not noticed." The devil is so cunning. He knows he could not induce a virtuous person to fall into a great sin because of the horror it inspires. What does he do? He proposes a venial offense; now one, now another until he gets the soul into an evil habit, for he knows the end result. Satan knows Scripture too, and can prove it from what he has been able to accomplish by making persons desire, at first, venially sinful things. Scripture says: "He that is unjust in that which is little will be unjust in that which is great" (Eccles. 19:1).

Pray earnestly today for grace to avoid venial sins. Examine your conscience daily on your commission of venial sins and resolve to do your utmost to avoid them.

Monday After the Second Sunday in Lent

THE kiss of Judas will ever remain the ultimate in base treachery. The name *Judas* has such a special odium that no one in his right mind would give that name to an infant. It is reserved for the foulest deed one can perform against a friend, a family, a nation, or a society. The act of kissing performed by Judas on the greatest Friend mankind ever had, beggars man's power of description. Oh, horrible perfidy!

It is related in Holy Scripture that one of the generals in David's army named Joab perpetrated a foul deed, in that upon meeting Amasa, who also commanded an army, he stooped forward to kiss him and that very moment thrust a dagger into his side and killed him. Solomon, David's famous son, when he succeeded to the throne, had Joab slain for his treachery.

Note how much more evil was Judas' act of treachery than was Joab's. Joab with a treacherous kiss murdered a fellow man; Judas by his kiss paved the way for the death of the Son of God. Joab on the other hand dispatched his victim in one quick thrust; Judas by his awful deed set the stage for the torture and painful death of his Lord and God.

It is related that when the assassins of Julius Caesar fell upon him with their daggers, the great conqueror of men and nations stood motionless, displaying not the slightest sign of emotion or fear. When Brutus, whom Caesar loved with the affection of a father, also approached and drew his dagger to strike his great benefactor, that blow caused Caesar more pain than all the other wounds, and he could not refrain from uttering those now famous words: "Thou too, Brutus, my son!" If Caesar was pained by the baneful treachery of his friend Brutus, how must the Son of God have felt when one of His own disciples betrayed Him to His enemies by a kiss.

Might the Master not have said: "You too, Judas, My son! Is this what I have merited for My kindness to you? Did I not choose you to be My follower, disciple, and apostle? Did I not wash your feet? Did I not give you My Body and Blood, Soul and Divinity as a food? O thankless, heartless Judas!"

Look into your heart today and see if you have ever betrayed your Master by mortal sin. Each time you prefer creatures to Christ you betray Him. Each time you choose sin to Christ's law, you betray Him. Spend some time today quietly thinking over the picture of Judas pressing his lips

to those of the sinless Christ. If you can identify yourself
in Judas, throw yourself quickly into the arms of your God
and beg His pardon.

Tuesday After the Second Sunday in Lent

WE NOTED in our last consideration that daggers were
used to murder Julius Caesar. The effect was just as tragic
as if the murderers had used swords. The smallness of the
instrument did not lessen the effects. In like manner, it
must be said of Judas that he did not lay violent hands on
Christ when he met Him in the Garden of Olives. No, he
did not seize or strike the Sacred Redeemer — he simply
kissed Him, but that kiss was more tragic than if he had
thrust a sword through the Sacred Heart of Christ.

Christ had been kissed before, but my, how different
were the circumstances and results! First, there were the
kisses of the Blessed Virgin Mary and St. Joseph. Who can
number the fond caresses that Mary must have showered
on the Infant Jesus as she nurtured and fondled Him
in her pure maternal arms? How often must not St. Joseph
have covered the Infant Countenance with tender paternal
affection?

Second, may we not conjecture that the Magi em-
braced the tiny Infant as Mary formally presented the
Infant God to the first of the Gentiles who came to pay
Him homage? Certainly, the act would be normal if not
imperative.

Third, it can hardly be imagined that the Holy Simeon and Anna present at the presentation in the temple, could have held the adorable Child of promise in their arms and not pressed their holy lips to the pink little hands of the long-sought Messias.

Fourth, we are certain from the text of Holy Scripture itself that the public sinner Mary Magdalen imprinted the kiss of contrite sorrow on the sacred feet of Christ, and arose from the encounter holier and greater than when she stooped to embrace her God.

Fifth, we are told that the great St. John the beloved disciple, rested his youthful head on the breast of the Master at the Last Supper. There is a Persian fable of a piece of clay made fragrant by lying on a rose: the perfume of the rose passed into the clay. So it was with John. He crept unto the bosom of the Master and his Master's spirit of love and gentleness passed into his life and transformed it.

Last, we have the awful picture of Judas pressing his lips to those of the Son of God, feigning friendship.

The lesson here is powerful. Those who approached Christ in love and veneration, in true penance and firm resolve, left His embrace renewed and strengthened. Those, like Judas, whose hearts are turned toward evil, may be very near Christ and not be holy in character. Judas was three years with Christ, heard His words, lived in the atmosphere of His love and remained unchanged. An empty bottle, hermetically sealed, may lie long in the ocean and continue perfectly dry within. A heart sealed to Christ's love may rest on His bosom for years and not be blessed. Only when the pure or contrite heart is opened to receive His grace, does closeness to Him sanctify.

Wednesday After the Second Sunday in Lent

ST. JOHN strikes an unusual note in his gospel relative to the incidents leading to Christ's arrest. The inspired writer put these words down for all posterity to read: "Now Judas, who betrayed him, also knew the place, since Jesus had often met there together with his disciples" (Jn. 18:2). Judas knew the place since Jesus "had often met there together with His disciples." These words give us but a glimpse of our Lord's habit of prayer. The deep quiet of the Garden of Olives was His oratory. Here the Son of God had been wont to pray. And there were other places, too, which were sacred resorts to Him. There were mountain tops, where He often spent whole nights in communion with His Father.

Our Lord's example of prayer teaches us that we should spend much time in prayer. Those people who are too busy to pray soon find their spiritual life on the wane. Not feeding their souls, they grow very lean. There can be no beautiful, strong, helpful Christian life without prayer.

Every tree has a root which people cannot see, but which in the secret, in the darkness, performs service for the tree without which the tree cannot live or bear fruit. What the root is to the tree, prayer is to the Christian. Prayer is the mighty weapon wherewith we can combat and put to flight our spiritual foes: the golden key wherewith we may unlock the inexhaustible treasury of the divine Heart and draw from It the graces we need for life's pilgrimage.

It is, moreover, the link which connects heaven with earth, which binds us to God: the mystical ladder Jacob saw, whereby our supplications ascend to Paradise and bring back to us its richest fruits. Prayer has a power, which, if we may so speak, forces the hand of God, an omnipotence which prevails even with the Most High.

Our Lord's example also teaches us the importance of regular habits of prayer. It was Christ Himself who said that without Him, left to ourselves, we are incapable of taking a single step in the way of salvation: "Without me you can do nothing" (Jn. 15:5). St. Paul tells us that without the assistance of grace we cannot so much as think a thought that is good. And the doctors of the Church teach us that, in the ordinary dealings of Providence, God does not give grace to those who do not ask for it. "Ask," He says, "and you shall receive." This is equivalent to saying: "I am always ready to bestow my grace upon you, on condition that you ask Me for it." Christ prayed forty days and nights on one occasion; He prayed before working His greatest miracles; He prayed in the Garden of Gethsemani; He prayed on Calvary. What does He do in the tabernacle but plead with His Father for us, to avert the chastisement due our sins? And seated on His throne at the right hand of the Father, Christ still makes intercession for us, He still is our great Advocate and Mediator.

How much time do you give to prayer? How well do you pray? Ask yourself these questions today and then make a firm resolve to do better. If Christ prayed — you must also pray and you have reason to pray more frequently and more fervently.

Thursday After the Second Sunday in Lent

IN ST. JOHN'S GOSPEL we read of a most striking incident in the initial steps of the arrest of Christ in the Garden of Gethesemani. Here are the exact words as the inspired writer penned them: "Jesus therefore knowing all that was about to come upon him, went forth and said to them: 'Whom do you seek?' They answered him, 'Jesus of Nazareth.' Jesus said to them, 'I am he.' Now Judas, who betrayed him, was also standing with them. When, therefore, he said to them: 'I am he,' they drew back and fell to the ground" (Jn. 18:5).

Christ had such a short time before been prostrated by intense mental and physical pain and He had prayed and prayed and prayed, and He was strengthened by an Angel, but now we see Him composed and confident as He stands before the armed soldiers. There was no weakness now. There was superb control. He simply said three words, "I am He," and the stalwart soldiers fell to the ground. Those who were so strong and arrogant lay prone, feeble, and impotent at Christ's feet.

The great St. Augustine does a masterly job of applying this scene to our individual lives. He says that if Christ acted in this manner when He was about to be arrested and judged by ungodly men, what will He be like when He is the Judge? If He displays such power at the moment He was about to be sentenced to death, what will His power be like when He stands in all His power and glory to judge each one of us?

If the simple words "I am He," spoken by the Redeemer of the world, had power enough in them to topple His enemies like tenpins or toy soldiers, imagine the effect of His voice when it is used to call us to account for our sins. St. Jerome asserts that when our Lord said to the soldiers: "I am He," a gleam of such fiery brightness flashed out of His eyes that the soldiers fell to the earth as if struck by lightning. In anticipation of that dread day of the judgment let us cast ourselves down at the feet of our Redeemer as a sign of sincere contrition and of repentance for our sins.

You will note that St. John says that "Judas, who betrayed Him, was also standing with them" (the soldiers) and presumably, he too was cast to the ground. The effect of this great miracle on Judas was *nil*. The habit of sin and impenitence had hardened the betrayer's heart and blinded him to the divinity of the Master.

St. Paul once felt the power of the voice of God. He was thrown from his horse at Damascus and he arose from the ground a new man. Judas was thrown to the ground in Gethsemani but he arose unchanged. What has this holy season of Lent done for you? Will you be closer to God, love Him more, and serve Him better because of your having done some voluntary penances, said more and better prayers, resolved to avoid the occasions of sin in persons, places, or things, or will you, like the betrayer, be unchanged, undisciplined, and unrepentant? Make your answer before you close this book today.

Friday After the Second Sunday in Lent

THE miracle that was worked to cast the enemies of Christ to the ground as He said "I am He," was done to prove that while the Son of God would not thwart the purposes of His sworn enemies who thirsted for His blood, the Master was resolved to do enough to render them inexcusable in putting Him to death. If they proceeded to arrest, torture, and crucify Christ, they would do it with the knowledge that they were acting against One who had divine power. The miracle was done to convince the enemies of Christ, led by the traitor Judas, that their imminent act was wrong, and that if they proceeded to culminate it, they would be accountable for it. The miracle went as far as to make those miserable who laid hands on the Son of God but not so far as to frustrate their impious design.

It scarcely ever happens that we commit any great sin without experiencing great resistance. This is particularly true of the first great sins in our life. The remorse, the degradation and the disillusionment is nearly enough to throw us to the ground, and the warning voice of conscience is like thunder in our soul. It is nearly a verity that after the first or the thousandth grave sin — but after one of them — there is a turning point in our life. We must not look to be kept prostrate on the ground for the mastery of conviction will release its strong hold, and we will gradually feel at liberty to arise — and then what shall we do? Paul was thrown to the ground but he arose saying to Jesus

— "Lord, what will Thou have me do?" Judas was struck to the ground but he arose only to renew his traitorous attack, to make fresh quest after Jesus whom he was determined to betray.

After any grave sin we must follow the example of Paul or that of Judas. If we rise from a serious sin determined to take another and another step toward sin, the likelihood is that the path will be smooth and we will be suffered to proceed without much protestation by our conscience, or by remorse. One thing we ought to fear, and that is to be left to sin undisturbed. The longer we remain in that state the worse the chances are for spiritual recovery.

When Christ's enemies laid hands upon His sacred Person, Peter drew his sword and lopped off the ear of Malchus, the servant of the High Priest. Christ told Peter to put away his sword and Scripture adds these words: " 'Bear with them thus far.' And he touched his ear and healed him" (Lk. 22:51).

Judas and the Roman soldiers, the Pharisees, Scribes, and Elders experienced two striking miracles in rapid succession — the strange power which hurled them to the ground, and the miraculous healing of the ear of the servant of the High Priest — but what was the effect upon Judas and the others who came to seize Christ? Nothing. They experienced miracles and remained adamant. Oh, the sad plight of those who betray Christ and those who crucify Him. St. Paul says that when men sin they crucify again to themselves the Son of God and make Him a mockery (Hebr. 6:6).

Never let a day pass without saying your three Hail Marys morning and night, adding this ejaculation: "Oh

Mary, my mother, preserve me from mortal sin this day (this night)."

Saturday After the Second Sunday in Lent

WHEN St. Peter drew the sword and made a thrust at the servant of the High Priest, Malchus, he, no doubt, meant to inflict a more telling wound than the mere severing of an ear. An instant before Peter's display of poor marksmanship, the Apostles had asked our Lord this question: "Lord, shall we strike with the sword?" (Lk. 22:49), but our Lord replied: "Put back thy sword into its place; for all those who take the sword will perish by the sword. Or dost thou suppose that I cannot entreat my Father, and he will even now furnish me with more than twelve legions of angels? How then are the Scriptures to be fulfilled, that thus it must happen?" (Mt. 26:52–54.) Before Christ had finished giving the above reply, Peter had already cut off the ear of the High Priest's servant.

Cornelius a Lapide, the famous commentator on Holy Scripture, asserts that Peter meant well in going to the defense of his Master, but that the Saint acted unwisely in that he did not permit himself to be guided by faith, rather he allowed himself to be carried away by his natural impetuosity. Therefore, Peter committed two faults: (1) against the will of Christ, inasmuch as he did not wait for Christ's answer, and (2) his use of the sword was in revenge rather than an act of defense. Besides this, Peter's act was one of great imprudence, for by it he surely could not expect to free Christ from the hands of so formidable an enemy. In fact, his act merely served to arouse the anger of the soldiery against the Saviour, and thus, exposed himself to the likelihood of a similar death.

Had Peter exercised his faith, he would have realized that, had Christ so desired it, He could have struck down His enemies, or hidden Himself as He had done before; in other words that, as the Son of God, He stood in no need of human defense. No doubt Christ wanted to teach the head of His Church on earth in particular, and all His followers in general, that they should meet malicious persons with meekness, patience, and charity. The general idea in all such matters is to show yourself meek, patient, and forbearing so that by such means, your enemies will find their anger softened.

We must follow this rule in daily life. St. Paul was wont to teach his followers this great lesson: "If it be possible, as far as in you lies, be at peace with all men. . . . Be not overcome by evil, but overcome evil with good" (Rom. 12:18, 21). We are encouraged to practice the virtue of forbearance by the prospect of a double gain for ourselves, in as far as, thereby, we become more Christlike and perform a meritorious act of self-denial, and an act of love for our enemies. Such conduct is profitable, too, for our neighbor who, at the sight of such virtue, is moved to reflect and is led into the way of salvation.

One sword we must take care not to use to destroy or harm others is our tongue. Examine yourself today on just how you act when unjustly accused or attacked.

Monday After the Third Sunday in Lent

WHEN the Apostles had asked our Lord whether they should draw their swords to defend Him from those who came to the entrance of the Garden of Olives to arrest Him, our divine Saviour posed a question of His own. He said: "Shall I not drink the cup that the Father has given me?" (Jn. 18:11), or in other words, "Must I not do the will of My Father?"

Those words must have struck the Apostles with particular force, for had they not heard this same Christ but a few short moments before ask His Father three separate times to let this same cup of agony pass from Him. If they heard our Lord ask that the chalice pass from Him, they also heard His humble submission: "Not My will but Thine be done."

The first Adam went wrong from the moment he refused to identify himself with God's design for him. Both Adam and Eve were called upon to accept God as the ruler of their hearts and actions and were given a test of their obedience and loyalty. They were asked, as we are all asked, to accept His law with their whole hearts and souls and by a free act of the will.

But Adam and Eve rejected God as their lawgiver and by their act of rebellion decided to be a law unto themselves — to do what they themselves chose and not what God chose for them. Our First Parents each in turn said:

"My will, not Thine be done," and in so doing, turned Paradise into a desert. The words of Christ spoken in the olive grove: "Thy will, not Mine be done" turned the desert into Paradise, and made Gethsemani the gate to heaven.

The Son of God, according to the Fathers, descended from heaven and clothed Himself with our flesh for three reasons: the one to redeem us by His Blood; the others to teach us by His doctrine the way to heaven, and finally to instruct us by His example.

Among many other instructions Christ has given us, one of the chief is that we should live in entire conformity to the will of God. This is a doctrine He taught us not only in words, when He bid us say to His eternal Father, "thy will be done on earth as it is in heaven" (Mt. 6:10), but what He has confirmed by His own example, because He Himself tells us, "I have come down from heaven, not to do my own will, but the will of him who sent me" (Jn. 6:38).

It is the testimony of millions who have tried to find peace of mind and happiness in this life by shunning the will of God, that they have tasted nothing but the bitter and persistent feelings of disillusionment, an agonizing sense of incompleteness, and a painful sense of frustration. These symptoms are seldom isolated, but usually hang together, one or the other predominating. Blessed is the person who can recognize the symptoms and straightaway start to return to God's plan for them.

Christ accepted the bitter cup offered by His Father and in so doing did the will of God. We must have the same trust in God. If God offers us a bitter chalice to drink to the dregs, let us do so with courage and faith. If God gives us a cup, it must be the very best that the wisest love can provide for us.

Pray — one our Father and Hail Mary today that you may always have faith enough to accept any type of cup God offers you. Say to God:

> If there should be some other thing
> Better than all the rest
> That I have failed to ask, I pray
> Give Thou the very best
> Of every gift that Thou dost deem
> Better than ought I hope or dream.

Tuesday After the Third Sunday in Lent

NO SOONER had Christ offered to drink the cup His Father offered Him than the soldiers laid their hands upon the gentle Saviour and the arrest was completed. At the very moment when Christ could have used the moral support of His disciples, Scripture records these sad words: "Then all the disciples left him and fled" (Mt. 26:56).

If we ever needed proof of the weakness of the Apostles, we need look no further than to the story of their desertion of Christ at the moment of His arrest. We can determine several reasons for the flight, a general one resulting from the inherent inconstancy of man, and the other resulting from adoption of false notions. The Apostles may have become infected with the notion that Christ's kingdom would be a material one and that if it was to be established

on this earth, they themselves would be in the best position
to be leaders. Had they not given proof on occasion of the
very false notion of the Kingdom of God, by disputing
among themselves about leadership? You know, there was
a good deal of pride in the group of ignorant fishermen
from the most insignificant provinces of the civilized world
who allowed themselves to gloat over the possibility of their
being autocratic leaders in the new kingdom.

It is quite possible too that Christ permitted the desertion without protest (1) to aggravate His sufferings, and (2)
to prove His love.

Keep before your mind, in studying the whole story
of the Passion, that Christ accepted the chalice offered Him
by His Father — a chalice filled to the brim with the sins
of the world. It is possible that the desertion of the Apostles was permitted that He might taste of every ingredient
of bitterness which is mingled in man's cup of woe, and
there are few things more bitter than being forsaken by
friends in an hour of need.

I am more inclined to believe that the desertion was
permitted to prove Christ's love for man. Who can ever
say that his sins are too great to be forgiven, or his heart
too depraved to be renewed? Only trust Him. His grace
is sufficient for you. Such a scene as the desertion of the
Apostles and yet His continued love for them, must encourage the worst of the backsliders to return to Him. Christ
did not disown His disciples, though they deserted Him
in His distress, but after His resurrection, He sent to them
by the faithful women, messages of tenderness and love.
"Go," said He to Mary Magdalen, "go to my brethren, and
say to them, 'I ascend to my Father and your Father, to

my God and your God'" (Jn. 20:17). And to the other women, Christ said: "Go, take word to my brethren that they set out for Galilee; there shall they see me" (Mt. 28:10). Go to our Lord in the tabernacle today and console Him for the number of times you have deserted Him. Tell Him how much you appreciate His efforts to make you realize the greatness of His love for, and mercy toward you. Pray especially today for the grace of final perseverance.

 ## Wednesday After the Third Sunday in Lent

IN THE accounts of the arrest of Christ, there is a particular and rather curious event that is mentioned by only one of the four Evangelists. The story is told by St. Mark in these words: "Then all his disciples left him and fled. And a certain young man was following him, having a linen cloth wrapped about his naked body, and they seized him. But leaving the linen cloth behind, he fled away from them naked" (Mk. 14:50).

Since St. Mark is the only Evangelist to record this circumstance, it is fairly well accepted by Scripture scholars that the young man referred to was St. Mark himself. It was common among the Evangelists to relate transactions in which they themselves took part without mentioning their own names. An added bit of proof that it was Mark himself who started out to follow Christ at the time of His false arrest and then deserted under the most embarrassing circumstance, is due to the fact that Mark did much the same thing after the resurrection. It was in his very marrow to be an enthusiastic starter but an easily discouraged person.

When St. Paul and St. Barnabas set out on their missionary journey they were attended by Mark. As long as they were sailing across the blue waters and as long as they were in the island of Cyprus, Mark stuck with them. Even while they traveled along the coast of Asia Minor, John Mark was their minister. But the moment they went up into the island countries, among the rocks and the mountain streams, among the robbers and crude natives, Mark left them. How tragically sad this whole missionary story would be if it had ended there. But it did not end there. Mark, by the grace of God and the example and counsels of Barnabas, rose to the occasion and went back to his missionary work in Cyprus and later we find him working with St. Paul, who called him in fond words — "My fellow laborer" (Phil. 24). The vacillating Mark became Mark the martyr, for he was martyred for the faith in Alexandria in Egypt.

Two powerful lessons come to us from the story of St. Mark. First, Mark in his youth may have followed Christ without counting the cost. He was impetuous. He dashed out to the assistance of Christ at the moment of His arrest. Not until he was seized by a soldier as a follower and associate of Christ did he realize that he of all the disciples had ventured too close and with too much false zeal and without the necessary accompanying virtue of prudence. It was not until Mark stood naked before His Master and heard the jeers of the soldiery who saw him make his escape that he realized his folly in relying on his own strength. It was then that he was emptied of his vanity.

The second lesson from this gospel story of Mark

should be one of great encouragement for sinners. Mark had made some good starts but he had failed miserably; yet he did not become discouraged even when the great St. Paul refused to trust him after his debacle of the missionary journey he had made in the company of Paul and Barnabas. Paul refused to take him on the second trip. Barnabas, on the other hand, had faith in him and he made good. If you have made good starts, if you have weakened in your Lenten resolutions, take them up again with courage. With men we are given but few chances. But God is patient and merciful. Forget the past and look with new hope to the future.

 ## Thursday After the Third Sunday in Lent

ST. LUKE gives us this cryptic description of Christ's arrest: "Now having seized him, they led him away to the high priest's house; but Peter was following at a distance" (Lk. 22:54).

Peter was deeply in earnest when he said at the Last Supper that if everyone else denied Christ he would never deny Him. Peter's high profession of loyalty and love partook somewhat of the nature of boasting. Doubtless, Peter knew his own weaknesses and he just had to make vows and assurances of fidelity in public and in a loud voice to convince himself. Such a mode of acting is the product and sign of a weak, unreliable character. I have heard of a little boat that carried such an immense whistle that it took all the steam to blow it, so, whenever it whistled, it stopped running. Peter was somewhat like that — he talked big, he boasted, and in so doing, he stopped thinking about his own weakness and dependence on God.

When Peter saw the soldiers seize Christ and take Him away, it must have struck him how much easier it was to make vows and protestations of loyalty and fidelity in the heavenly atmosphere of the Upper Room than it was to make protestations amid the awesomeness of the Garden of Gethsemani and the excitement of the Judgment Hall.

But Peter was such a bundle of contradictions. It is worthy of note that Peter fled when Christ was arrested but then, soon after the senseless and useless panic, it appears that at least two of the Apostles rallied their wavering courage and came back to Christ. The two were John and Peter. Perhaps the courage of John served to strengthen Peter. Certainly on this occasion John's zeal and courage outweighed Peter's. John did his best to make up for his temporary defection by edging his way directly through all obstacles into the very apartment where Jesus had been taken for trial. John "entered with Jesus . . . but Peter was standing outside at the gate" (Jn. 18:15, 16).

To what may we ascribe Peter's initial flight? It may not have been simply the sudden fright of alarm but rather because his piety, at that period of his history, was fashioned more by feeling than by principle. He was the man who grew ecstatic on the mount of the Transfiguration and proposed that Jesus and himself and the others never quit that great place. No one can hope to stand firm in time of stress or opposition if his or her piety has been nurtured only in tender hours of emotional enjoyment. Christ Himself announced the basis for His friendship and service when He said: "He who does not carry his cross and follow me, cannot be my disciple" (Lk. 14:27). Peter failed because he placed too much confidence in his own strength, and he failed even more miserably when he abandoned the cause he had espoused.

Ask yourself these questions today. Whom do you follow? The obligation you are under is to follow Christ closely and so learn from Peter's plight that, if the consequences of following Christ afar off be so dreadful, what must be the consequence of not following Him at all?

Friday After the Third Sunday in Lent

IT WAS about midnight when our Lord reached the palace of Annas, the high priest who, with the Pharisees who had assembled there, was impatiently awaiting the arrival of the detested Nazarene with feelings of malicious pleasure and bitter scorn. The Jews did right in bringing Christ to Annas. Legally, he was the high priest, and held that high office by right for life. The truth is that, after only some nine years in office, he was deposed by the Roman authorities. He had had various successors, each of whom served but a short time until Caiphas came into Roman favor and took the office of high priest, a position, Josephus Flavius says, he purchased at a high price. This interloper Caiphas had occupied the position of High Priest for sixteen years when Christ was arrested.

It must be noted that Caiphas was the son-in-law of Annas — and that whenever, in Scripture, the two names are mentioned together, Annas takes precedence. Annas, therefore, was the leading figure in the conspiracy hatched against the Master, and upon him primarily rests the crime of deicide.

For blind men to be fair critics of Michelangelo, for deaf men to be fair judges of the musical works of Verdi, for moles to be fair critics of sunshine would be more conceivable than the possibility of men like Annas and Caiphas being fair judges of Jesus Christ! How could such cruel, base sinners ever be able to understand the sinless Son of God made Man? Besides their bias, there was natural unfitness, there was unfairness from the fact that they were desperate conspirators, plotting against the Messias to curry favor with the Jews and the Romans.

Before this mock trial begins let us look at the Prisoner — Jesus Christ. See Him as He stands bound before His judges and the mob who had dragged Him from the Garden of Olives. He had gone through the horrible agony in the Garden of Gethsemani; He was weak and exhausted from that frightful struggle; He had experienced the horrible emotional strain of seeing one of His own followers betray Him to His enemies; He had seen His other friends desert Him; and He had been dragged through the streets to His mock trial. The Son of God who had been so faithful to the Mosaic Law was to be a victim of its nonobservance. You see, the Mosaic law prohibited trial by night or on the vigil of a festival day. Nevertheless, Christ was dragged before the tribunal in the very middle of the night: indeed the night preceding the great Jewish solemnity.

Honor with every power of your soul and body the great humility of Christ, the God of infinite greatness and majesty, who allows Himself to be arrested, bound, and led captive by the very men whom, but a few moments before, He had overthrown and cast on the ground by a few simple words from His lips. Honor Christ's charity too — charity that placed Him a captive in the power of the Jews in order to deliver you and me from the captivity of the devil — charity that thrust Him into prison to save you and me from the prison of hell. Go to the gentle Prisoner of the tabernacle today, for He is right here our voluntary Prisoner, where He remains night and day out of love for us. Ask yourselves if you have resembled those who arrested Christ, if you have ever taken our Lord out of His voluntary prison house in order, by your unworthy communion, to drag Him to Calvary and crucify Him anew?

 ## Saturday After the Third Sunday in Lent

WHILE Christ was being arraigned before Annas, the high priest, Peter mingled with the crowd in the courtyard. A fire was soon kindled to ward off the cold of the night, and Peter drew closer and sat down with the rest. St. Luke remarks that a certain maidservant saw him sitting at the blaze, and after gazing upon him she said: "This man too was with Him." But he denied Him, saying, "Woman, I do not know him" (Lk. 22:56–57). St. Mark adds that Peter "went outside into the vestibule; and the cock crowed" (Mk. 14:68).

If there ever was a Jekyll and Hyde it was Peter. At the Last Supper, Peter was superb. He was fervent, generous, and brave. Hear him as he says to Christ: "I will lay down my life for thee." Jesus answered him: "Wilt thou lay down thy life for me? Amen, amen, I say to thee, the cock will not crow before thou dost deny me thrice" (Jn. 13:37, 38). Certainly, Peter was brave, if foolhardy, in drawing his sword to defend Christ against the soldiers who came to seize Him in the Garden of Gethsemani. Now, look at the other Peter in the court of the high priest. What a pitiful change! The closest friend of the Messias takes his place in the midst of Christ's enemies. He sits around the fire with them. A maidservant taunts him about being a friend, associate, and companion of Jesus of Nazareth, and hear Peter: "Woman, I do not know Him."

For our instruction and warning, note the steps Peter took to this dismal state wherein he could deny Christ. First, Peter was too self-confident. When Christ forewarned him, he resented the Master's foretelling, and declared that though others might deny Christ, he would never do so. Whenever we grow boastful we are in peril. Safety lies in a consciousness of our own weakness and in implicit trust in God.

Next, Peter slept in the Garden of Olives when he should have watched and prayed. Again, Peter was rash in drawing his sword in the garden. That incident made him nervous and afraid of recognition. He had a right to fear recognition lest he should be arrested for his assault on the servant of the high priest. Still another step toward the denial resulted from the fact that Peter followed Christ from afar. Following Christ at a distance is always perilous. It shows a weakening attachment and a trembling loyalty. The only way to follow Christ is by thorough, unwavering devotion and wholehearted consecration, no matter what the cost. The final step that led Peter to his denial of Christ lay in the fact that he sat down among the servants of the high priest. He had gone among them in order to hide his relation to Christ. The only safe way for any follower of Christ is to disclose, unequivocally and nobly, complete attachment and discipleship.

Learn from this to avoid beginnings. The time to check yourselves is at the outset of your defections.

 ## Monday of the Fourth Week in Lent

WHILE Peter was making his first denial of Christ, the Sacred Redeemer was standing bound before Annas. My, how delighted Annas was that the Jews had brought Jesus first to him rather than to his son-in-law Caiphas, who was high priest because the Romans had unlawfully given him that post. De facto for all intents and purposes, although deposed, Annas was by Mosaic Law the real high priest. Indeed this whole affair may have been Annas' idea; he may have thought that if he condemned Christ as a threat to Roman power and rule, his own position might be made stronger in the minds of the Roman authorities. But conjecture is time wasting. The point was, Christ was standing before Annas. He hated the Galilean and was happy that he would be given the high privilege of humiliating Him.

"The high priest therefore questioned Jesus concerning his disciples, and concerning his teaching. Jesus answered him: 'I have spoken openly to the world; I have always taught in the synagogue and in the temple, where all the Jews gather, and in secret I have said nothing. Why dost thou question me? Question those who have heard what I spoke to them; behold, these know what I have said.'

"Now when he had said these things, one of the attendants who was standing by struck Jesus a blow, saying, 'Is that the way thou dost answer the high priest?' Jesus answered him, 'If I have spoken ill, bear witness to the evil; but if well, why dost thou strike me?'" (Jn. 18:19-23.)

Note the great clarity with which Christ answered the high priest. First he made it clear that He had no secret doctrines and no plots to contrive. Second, Christ's answer made an old truth evident in that it was irregular and illegal to compel a man to witness against himself. "Question those who heard what I spoke to them" — in other words, "produce witnesses against Me."

Annas was trapped, and his pride was injured. It was to relieve him of his embarrassment that the attendant struck our Lord with his fist in the face. Behold your Lord and your God staggering beneath the pain of that cruel blow and see His precious blood flow from His mouth and nose. The blow was senseless because it was struck by one who wanted to gain the favor of the high priest and because it drew ridicule on Christ from the bystanders. "Alas," cries St. Chrysostom, "is our God to be received with buffets! Grow dark ye heavens, with horror. O earth, tremble at such a deed. Let each of us bewail our sins, for they caused that cruel blow to be struck."

St. Chrysostom writes that it was the same Malchus whom Peter had struck in the garden of Gethsemani, who struck Christ so cruelly in the presence of the High Priest. Oh, the power of Christ's gentle answer to the one who struck Him! The calm, sweet answer, the patience, the absolute control did what the miracle of the healing of his ear could not do. St. John Chrysostom further affirms expressly that the grace of God entered Malchus' soul with the words: "Why dost thou strike Me?" and his eyes were opened to the light of divine truth.

The next time you are tempted to sin bring those words of Christ to mind. "Why dost thou strike Me?" Each time we sin gravely, we not only strike Him, we crucify anew our loving Saviour. Say with St. Dominic Savio — "Death rather than mortal sin."

Tuesday of the Fourth Week in Lent

YOU will recall that Annas was the lawful but deposed high priest, and the Jews made a great point of the fact by bringing Christ before him rather than before the unlawful hand-picked Roman choice, Caiphas.

Our Lord, by His direct and clear answers, disarmed Annas completely, and so, to save face, Annas directed that Christ be arraigned before Caiphas. Hence the Saviour was bound and sent off to the home of the quisling Caiphas, where the Scribes and the elders had gathered. Here the ordeal was much worse for Christ. One has only to picture the rage and deceitfulness etched on the faces of Caiphas and his council to know how biased such a court session would be. He would certainly never find justice or mercy here.

Under the guise of making it legal, the Elders and Scribes had hastily called the whole Sanhedrin, whose full complement was seventy-two members, representing equally the three groups of priests, Scribes, and Elders. The function of this council was to take cognizance of grave matters of a doctrinal, judicial, or administrative character affecting the Jewish religion and nation. They had neglected nothing, for they had even secured the services of witnesses. When any good lawyer examines the records of the trial of Christ before the Sanhedrin it is obvious that the witnesses contradicted each other and, time and again, contradicted themselves (cf. Mk. 14:56). For instance, two witnesses stepped up before the court and said: "He said, and we heard Him say: 'I can destroy the temple and in three days I can rebuild it.'"

One witness said that Christ's words were: "I can destroy," the other said that His words were: "I shall destroy." The important thing is that St. John gave us the exact words of Christ, which were "Destroy this temple, and in three days, I will raise it up" (3:19). We know, and they did too, that Christ did not mean the material temple in Jerusalem, but His own body.

Oh, how wicked men can be to falsify Christ's own words and use them against Him! For any one to presume to think that he could or would destroy the Jewish Temple in Jerusalem was the very handle of blasphemy Christ's enemies wanted to hang on Him. Consider this base deceit in our Lord's enemies who concealed their hatred and envy under the cloak of zeal for God's glory. Ask yourself this question, if you have not sometimes under the mask of anxiety for God's glory, vented on your neighbor sentiments of anger and aversion. Ask yourself whether or not you have been guilty of uncharitable judgments and slander, making it seem as if you were acting solely in the interest of truth. Ask yourself if you have not sometimes put words in the mouth of a person you disliked to make him out to be evil in the eyes of others.

Remember, too, that all this took place in the house of the high priest. Ask yourself, whether you have always reserved for God's house the respect and reverence it deserves. Christ's enemies found no hardship in gathering there at midnight to abuse and mock the Son of God. How often have you not resented the few moments you are required to give to the worship and love of your Prisoner God in the tabernacle?

 ## Wednesday of the Fourth Week in Lent

WHILE our Lord was appearing before Caiphas, Peter had followed the Master from the home of Annas. With his usual abandon, Peter went right into the courtyard. You see, Caiphas' home followed the usual style of such houses. It was arranged about two courtyards, surrounded by porticoes, onto which the windows and doors opened. The first courtyard was reserved for the servants and workmen, the second, raised above the first by a few steps and entered through a massive door reserved for the use of the high priest, before which was situated the great meeting hall of the Sanhedrin. The gate at the entrance to the house was usually guarded by a female slave.

For the second time that fateful night, Peter was recognized as a follower of the Messias, and another maidservant said to those who had gathered around: "This man was also with Jesus of Nazareth," and Peter, Scripture says, "denied with an oath, 'I do not know the man!'" (Mt. 26:72.) Shortly thereafter someone else saw Peter, and said: "Thou, too, art one of them." But Peter said, "Man, I am not" (Lk. 22:58).

What a pitiful spectacle was Peter! He loved his Master, but strange to relate, despite all his love he could not rise to the occasion and confess Him. His impetuosity constantly placed him in danger. Peter lied when he denied knowing Christ the first time he was accused of it. He lied again, as we have just seen, when he was questioned the second time, but he somehow knew his lie was not very convincing so he had to emphasize it with an oath.

He who tells a lie is not sensible to how great a task he undertakes, for he is usually forced to tell many more lies to maintain the first one. Indeed, the ways of falsehood are perplexed and tangled. Oh, if Peter had had the courage of St. Anthimus! It is related that the holy Bishop of Nicomedia would not allow the soldiers who were sent to arrest him and who were enjoying his hospitality, to save him by a lie. He preferred to suffer martyrdom rather than be the cause of a lie in his behalf.

Learn from this second awful denial by Peter of his God,

not to rely on your own strength to keep you from falling into sin. Had Peter taken a good estimate of his own weakness, he would never have exposed himself to temptation for the second time. Learn not to rely on past conduct as a safeguard against future falls. Peter was under no stress when he openly confessed earlier in his ministry his belief in the divinity of Christ, saying "Thou art the Christ, the Son of the living God" (Mt. 16:16). Under the taunting gaze of a maidservant, and in the face of possible arrest as an associate of the Messias, he found himself void of his former courage. Peter counted too much upon himself; and so he fell, as everyone falls who trusts solely in his own strength and exposes himself rashly to danger.

Learn, finally, that Peter's repeated protestations of fidelity made the evil of denial more grievous. It is a greater sin for one who has publicly declared his love for Christ to prove disloyal to Him, than for one who has never made such a profession.

 ## Thursday of the Fourth Week in Lent

THE poor dupes who had been hoping to curry the favor of the Elders by offering to act as witnesses against Christ, no doubt received naught for their pains but the contempt of their leaders. They had botched the job in relating that they personally had heard Christ say "He would destroy the temple and in three days rebuild it." Scripture records the court session as follows: "For while many bore false witness against Him, their evidence did not agree" (Mk. 14:56).

The charge was so nebulous, and the witnesses so damaging to the cause for which the Sanhedrin had been assembled that Caiphas decided to retrieve what he could from the farce. He stood up, and said to our Lord: " 'Dost thou make no answer to the things these men prefer against thee?' But he kept silence and made no answer" (Mt. 14:60, 61).

There is a silence which is often more eloquent than words, and means more than any words, and speaks volumes to the heart. Such, for example, is the silence when the heart is too full for utterance and the organs of speech are choked by the overwhelming surge of emotions. Such also is the silence of the wise man challenged to speak by those whom he feels unworthy of his words. The man who can stand and listen to ignorance, venomous bigotry, or personal hurt or insult addressed to him in an angry, insolent, offensive spirit, and offers no reply, exerts a far greater power over the mind of his assailant than he could by words, however forceful. Such was the silence Christ now maintained in the house of the High Priest, Caiphas.

When one's life and works are above reproach, these are the best defense against those who would do us harm. The accusations against Christ were false and frivolous and His silence was a sufficient and powerful reply. It is reported of Titus Vespasian that when anyone spoke ill of him he was wont to say that he was above false reports: and if they were true, he had more reason to be angry with himself than with the person who started the story.

When we bear wrongs patiently, we benefit not ourselves only but also our fellow man; we prevent him from going to greater lengths, and make it easier to bring him to a sense of his wrongdoing. Christ's silence was magnificent. He showed us a marvelous example of restraint under the most trying circumstances. How solemnly His silence rebukes the chatter of the false witnesses before the Elders of the Sanhedrin. The anvil breaks a host of hammers by quietly bearing the blows. Christ's silence broke the spirit of his accusers.

Christ during His life on earth gave a number of examples of silence. For instance he was silent in the presence of the Canaanite woman. Scripture says "He answered her not a word" (Mt. 15:23). He was silent when the accusers threw at His feet the woman taken in adultery (Jn. 8:4), but His most glorious silence was when He Himself was accused falsely.

How do you act when others accuse you wrongly? Are you oversensitive about your honor? St. Francis de Sales tells us that only when grave and disgraceful crimes are imputed to us, such as we cannot allow ourselves to be charged with, should we take steps to clear ourselves. Ask our dear Lord to give you the courage to be silent like He was, when accused unjustly.

Friday of the Fourth Week in Lent

THE patient Christ broke His silence to answer the High Priest's direct question couched in these words: "I adjure thee by the living God that thou tell us whether thou art the Christ, the Son of God" (Mt. 26:63). To that question

Christ replied: " 'I am. And you shall see the Son of Man sitting at the right hand of the Power and coming with the clouds of heaven.' But the high priest tore his garments and said, 'What further need have we of witnesses? You have heard the blasphemy. What do you think?' And they all condemned him as liable to death" (Mk. 14:61-64).

How audacious of Caiphas to dare ask the Son of God to answer him under oath! Yet Christ accepted that challenge even in the face of certain death and answered in the affirmative. And how was Christ's testimony received? You must notice, if you study this scene even casually, that it mattered little to Caiphas how Christ answered that question. When Caiphas asked the question "Art thou the Christ?" was he prepared to accept the evidence? Let us see. Naturally, our Lord could not lie, but just suppose He had said "No!" In that case He would have been called an impostor and condemned to death as a blasphemer. But now, when He answered "I am" to Caiphas' question, was there the least tendency on the part of the high priest to accept the testimony? No. Instead, Caiphas rent his garments and cried out that all had heard the blasphemy he heard and then proceeded to lead the Sanhedrin into calling for Christ's death.

No matter how the gentle Christ had answered Caiphas' loaded question, He would have heard the same outcry — "death to the blasphemer."

Unfortunately, the closed mind did not die with Caiphas. Many people today are more like Caiphas than they are like Christ. They have assumed a spirit of opposition to evident truth, and thereby, preclude any evidence from producing a lasting effect.

Our Holy Mother the Church teaches us through the Holy Scripture and the living word of her priests that when we begin to love the world we begin to dislike religion. When we begin to worship money we cease to worship God as we should, with our whole heart, our whole mind, our whole soul, and all our strength. When we begin to love houses of pleasure we begin to dislike the house of prayer. When we seek godless, irreligious friends and companions, we soon find good people dull and boring. The testimony is evident and copious but we often close our minds to its force and, like Caiphas, we preclude the evidence in favor of prayerful, upright moral lives and gradually banish Christ from our lives, homes, and actions.

Christ spoke the truth in answer to Caiphas' question: "Art thou the Christ, the Son of the living God?" when He replied "I am." Why do we doubt the truth of Christ's words then when He says: "Unless you do penance you shall all likewise perish" (Lk. 13:3); or when He says: "Except you eat the flesh of the Son of Man and drink his blood you shall not have life in you" (Jn. 6:54); or when He says: "Everyone that hath left house, or brothers, or sisters, or father, or mother, or wife, or children, or lands, for my name's sake, shall receive a hundredfold, and shall possess life everlasting" (Mt. 19:29)? Caiphas had closed his heart so Christ's words meant nothing to him. Have you closed your heart to Christ's words? Do you listen to your conscience? Do you take lightly the inspirations aroused by sermons and pious reading? Mark well these words of God: "My Son, forget not my law, and let thy heart keep my commandments. For they shall add to thee length of days and years of life and peace" (Prov. 3:1–2).

Saturday of the Fourth Week in Lent

PETER moves in and out of the scenes of Christ's trials with regularity. Recovering from his first panic at the arrest of Christ, from which he fled, he managed to recover enough of his bravado to follow Christ at a safe distance when the Saviour was taken to the home of Annas. Here he was content to remain outside until John used his influence to get a maid at the gate to permit Peter to enter the outer court. It was here that Peter first denied he was a follower of the Messias.

When Christ was led bound to the house of the high priest Caiphas, Peter followed, and managed to get a place near the glowing fire in the outer court where he was spotted as a stranger and again accused of being a disciple of Jesus of Nazareth. Again Peter denied this and did so with a very unconvincing reply couched in forceful language: "I do not know the man" (Mt. 26:72).

It was about an hour later now and Peter had returned from the gate, where he had gone after the second denial. He may have heard the shouts of the assembled Sanhedrin crying out in mock indignity that Christ was guilty of blasphemy and was worthy of death, for the sacred writer says that Simon Peter was standing warming himself (Jn. 18:25) when "one of the bystanders came up and said to Peter: 'Surely thou also art one of them, for even thy speech betrays thee.' Then he began to curse and to swear that he did not know the man" (Mt. 26:73, 74).

You will note that Peter made his three denials flatly and peremptorily. He made a triple denial and this indicates revolution. He made the denials not before one witness but before many, and so gave scandal, for no doubt there were some of the common people who maintained some reverence for the great wonder-worker Christ, and Peter's denial of his Lord and Master may have hardened them and the scandal may have prevented some of them from going forward to testify in Christ's favor.

It is worthy of note, too, that Peter remained in the outer courts of both Annas' and Caiphas' homes. He mingled with the servants and accepted their hospitality, shared the same fire, and sat with them. True, he did quit their company once and go to the gate but he quickly returned. Many persons step out of the midst of sin but hang about its courts. They themselves would not be outrageous sinners but retain a taste for sin. They may not openly commit sins against the Sixth Commandment but they harbor bad thoughts and desires and use impure language. They are not drunkards themselves, but they keep company with loose-livers and wild scatter-brained individuals and groups. Keep ever before you the picture of Peter denying his God. Peter was a great and forward disciple of Christ, full of zeal, who prayed, professed his great devotion to Christ, and who drew his sword in Christ's defense, but now behold him denying that same Christ before a few servants and soldiers. Great is the force of evil company to pervert even a godly mind. As the body is infected by pestilential air, so the soul is infected by the contagion of bad company.

Ask yourself today if your friends are all of a high type

and beyond reproach. Do you always give your friends good example? Do you profess Christ to your friends or are you sometimes afraid to make the Sign of the Cross and say Grace before and after meals in their presence? Are you afraid to visit a church when you are with friends? Ask St. Peter today to pray for you that you may never deny God by word or deed.

 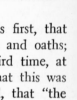

Monday After Passion Sunday

IT IS noteworthy that Holy Scripture records first, that Peter emphasized his third denial with curses and oaths; and second, that the cock crowed for the third time, at which instant it suddenly dawned on Peter that this was the very thing Christ had foretold; and third, that "the Lord turned and looked upon Peter and he remembered the word of the Lord, how He said: 'Before a cock crows, thou wilt deny me thrice,' and Peter went out and wept bitterly" (Lk. 22:61–62).

There is a powerful lesson to be drawn from the fact that Peter endeavored to strengthen his third denial by cursing and swearing. Peter had been and was a fisherman. Before being converted and called to the apostolate, he had been a man of strong language. The three years with the gentle Christ had weaned him away from that habit. He was certain, no doubt, that he had mastered control of his tongue and language. Certainly the companionship with Christ had done much, but it had not done all. The "old man" was still alive and the "new man" was weak, and so the battle ensued and the old habits were quick to return. From this, we may learn that the fact that we have not committed sins of habit for a long time does not mean that they are completely eradicated. We must ever be on the watch and pray that we may not fall into them in times of temptation or stress.

Next, note that it was not until the cock crowed thrice that Peter remembered the words of our Lord. It is hard to understand why Peter did not realize what was happening after he heard the crow of the rooster after the first denial. And why did Peter not remember Christ's prediction after the second denial? No, it took three denials and a heartbreaking glance from the gentle Saviour to touch Peter's heart, and to recall to mind the words of the Lord concerning Peter's vain boasting about fidelity.

Learn from this that sin deadens the heart to every voice and blinds the eye to sin. From your own experience perhaps you can recall occasions when you yourself were so attached to sin that the warnings of your parents, the stirring sermons of retreats and parish missions left you cold and unmoved.

It may well have been that the gentle Saviour looked tenderly at you too as He did at Peter. How wonderful is our God, who at a time when He Himself was about to be sentenced to the cruel death of the cross, thought of His poor weak Apostle, and forgot Himself and His own condition to cast a tender, merciful, understanding glance at His follower. "He spoke with His eye," says Erasmus. The power that went with that look struck Peter's heart. Without the calm sovereignty of that look, without its accompanying pitying kindness, Peter might well have followed in the footsteps of Judas.

Walk the Way of the Cross today and beg of the gentle Christ to let His sacred healing glance fall upon you as it fell upon Simon, the Cyrenian, St. Veronica, and the women who wept as He passed. Catch His eye as He falls under the cross and beg of Him to preserve you from despair.

Tuesday After Passion Sunday

THE fact that Christ looked at Peter as the cock crowed for the third time is recorded only in St. Luke's Gospel, but Luke, Matthew, and Mark all record that "Peter went out and wept bitterly." That look of the Master cut Peter to the quick. As Moses' rod once struck the rock and water flowed, so the gentle glance of Christ caused Peter's heart to overflow. That heart was singularly touched, and the fear-frozen memories thawed into penitential tears.

Peter's conversion followed a fine pattern. First, you will notice that Peter went out — he left the place and persons who occasioned his shameful denial of our Lord. There can never be any true and lasting conversion until, and unless, we are determined to avoid the occasions of sin — that is, any person, place, or thing that may cause us to fall. We will notice, too, that when Peter took himself away from the evil company he was in, he was able to look at Christ and Christ at him. Whoever wants to cleave to God must sever himself from God's enemies. Avoid, therefore, evil companions.

Consider next that Peter's repentance was immediate. He did not put off his conversion and repentance. Many of us desire to avoid sin and be really converted but, like St. Augustine, say in folly "but not yet." We seem to put more than ordinary trust in becoming holy when our vices have forsaken us. We dwell too often on the easy conversion of the Good Thief, but as St. Augustine warns: "Christ pardoned one thief on the cross to show that such things are possible, but only one to show it to be very rare."

Let us ask ourselves why Peter wept. First, in his quiet moments he realized that he had denied his Lord. Have we not all at one time or another denied our Lord? If you have deliberately missed Mass; given scandal or bad example; resisted God's will or that of His Church — then take your place with Peter.

The second thing that brought Peter to penitential tears was the thought of the excellence of the Lord whom he had denied. Have you thought seriously of how much Christ has done for you, the graces He has merited for and showered upon you — the home, the health, the advantages He has provided for you?

Third, Peter remembered the position in which the Lord had placed him — converting, befriending, and calling him to His apostolate. Has Christ not placed us all in positions of honor and trust as Christians? Do we not call ourselves Christians, followers of Christ? Yet not only have we not always followed Christ, but we may well have led souls away from Christ by our bad example and sins.

Fourth, Peter recollected that he had been forewarned. Have we not sinned against the light and with full knowledge and full consent in grave matters? Oh, have we not all frequently resisted the Holy Ghost, our conscience, and the warnings of our parents, teachers, and the Church? Think about your wanderings, backslidings, and your small progress on the road to perfection!

Peter fell dreadfully, but by repentance rises sweetly. A look of love melts him into tears. Clement notes that Peter was so repentant that all his life after, when he heard a rooster crow, he would fall upon his knees, and weeping, would beg pardon for his sins. Beg of Peter to teach you the necessity and the way of true repentance.

 Wednesday After Passion Sunday

THE charge of blasphemy was hurled against Christ by Caiphas, and, after rending his garments — a ritualistic sign of finality — the high priest left the gathering of the Sanhedrin and the group dispersed leaving Christ to the sport of the soldiers. St. Luke puts it this way: "And the men who had him in custody began to mock him and beat him. And they blindfolded him and kept striking his face, and asking him, saying, Prophesy, who is it that struck thee?' And many other things they kept saying against him, reviling Him" (Lk. 22:63–65). St. Matthew adds that they "spat in his face and buffeted him" (Mt. 26:67).

There is hardly another scene in the whole terrible story of the Passion that compares with the one in which mere mortals taunted, mimicked, maltreated, and grossly insulted the veritable Son of God. No artist has ever tried to portray this vicious scene. We have paintings by famous artists of the flagellation, the crowning of thorns, and the crucifixion but none has dared to depict the scene wherein Christ was so basely treated in the home of the high priest Caiphas in the early hours of the morning following His arrest. Not one artist has dared portray men spitting into the adorable face of God. It shocks even one's imagination to conjure up such a picture.

The worst criminal would have been given time to rest before his arraignment before Roman authorities on the morrow. He would have been given bread and water, but not Christ. Small comforts were denied Him. He was bound to a small pillar by iron chains and bound in such a position as not to be able to stand erect or fall to the hard floor. In His darkened hour in the garden of Olives an angel came to comfort Him, but here, He saw naught but the cruel soldiers mocking and reviling Him. Even His enemies were shut off from Him by the dirty cloth with which He was blindfolded. "Thou dost claim to be a Prophet," they shouted. "Well, tell us who is striking Thee." You say You are a king — well, You will be crowned a king tomorrow. All the time they reviled and mocked Him, the soldiers kept striking, kicking, and spitting into His face.

Who is it that endures such torments? It is Jesus Christ, the Son of God, at whose birth the angels sang: "Glory to God in the highest," the same one of whom God the Father said: "This is my beloved Son, in whom I am well pleased" (Mt. 3:17). What has happened that He is so abandoned and so insulted? Let us say here and now that no one compelled Christ to undergo this torment. He offered Himself of His own free will to pay the ransom for your sins and mine. Ask yourself if there is or has ever been any one who has loved you enough to suffer thus for you? To whom then does your love belong? Christ bore the heavy chains to free us from the galling chains of our passions and sins. He bore a prison sentence that we might be freed from the eternal prison of hell. He endured the spitting in his face to repair for the awful insults men have offered, and do and will offer His eternal Father.

Go to your Christ in His new prison — the tabernacle — and beg pardon for the insults you have heaped on Him by your sins. If you condemn in your heart the foolish men who insulted our Lord during the Passion, think how much worse your insults are since the soldiers were pagans but you are a child of God and a follower of Christ.

Thursday After Passion Sunday

THE soldiers, tired from making sport of the chained Christ took some rest, but the bruised, besmirched, disheveled, humiliated Saviour stood in the chill of the early dawn. As the sun was rising, the chief priests, the Scribes, and the whole Sanhedrin held a secret meeting. Strange, isn't it, how willing and easy men rise to do evil, while the doing of good seems so irksome? The sacred writers do not relate what took place at that meeting except to say that they "took counsel together against Jesus in order to put Him to death" (Mt. 27:1).

The secret meeting was soon concluded and a public

session was instigated. Try to imagine the scene. See Christ in His deplorable state being dragged into the large meeting room. See Him meet every glance with a searching look. He was God, and, as God, knew what had transpired at the secret session and He could read, too, the hearts of His enemies. Why would they bother to go through the formalities of a second investigation, since, certainly, they were not searching for the truth. They had already taken "counsel together" against Him, "in order to put Him to death."

It was because Christ knew their thoughts that He said in reply to the question: "If thou art the Christ, tell us?" "If I tell you, you will not believe me; and if I question you, you will not answer me, or let me go. But henceforth, the Son of Man will be seated at the right hand of the power of God." And they all said: "Art thou, then, the Son of God?" He answered, "You yourselves say that I am"; and they said: "What further need have we of witness? For we have heard it ourselves from his own mouth" (Lk. 22:66–71). "And they bound him and led him away, and delivered him to Pontius Pilate the procurator" (Mt. 27:2).

When Caiphas put that loaded question directly to Christ: "Tell us, art thou the Christ?" Our Lord replied in kind. Remembering what abuse He had suffered when that question had been asked at the first meeting of the Sanhedrin a few hours earlier, our Lord said: "If I tell you, you will not believe me, and if I question you, you will not answer me, or let me go." Here the Master was clearly referring to the prophecies of the Old Testament regarding the Messias, which they, as scholars and teachers, were supposed to know well, and which, if they would only open their eyes, could see clearly were fulfilled and verified in Him. The high priest and the Sanhedrin had but one single thought and that was not the fulfillment of the prophecies but the destruction of Christ. The merciful Christ in an endeavor to impress His enemies with the salutary fear of the consequences of their unjust action, added as He did at His first trial — "you shall see the Son of Man sitting on the right hand of the power of God," alluding clearly to the final judgment of all men, where true justice would prevail.

How often have we not all heard the Ten Commandments, listened to sermons, read books, studied Christ's counsels and with our hearts set on sinning, closed our mind and conscience to the voice of God pleading with us to keep His law. How often may some of us have prayed half in earnest to know our vocation, to which prayer Christ could say in answer: "If I shall tell you, you will not believe me, and if I question you, you will not answer me"?

Will you not go to Christ in His tabernacle today, and appease His wounded heart for the indignities heaped upon Him before Caiphas and the Sanhedrin? Tell Him how ready you are to do His will in all things.

 ## Friday After Passion Sunday

THE farcical trials before the high priest were over. Christ had been found guilty of blasphemy because He said He

was the Son of God. This, under the Jewish law was punish-
able by death, but since the sentence could not be carried
out without the consent of the Romans, Christ would
have to appear before Pontius Pilate who was the Roman
governor or procurator at that time. When word of Christ's
condemnation reached the unfortunate Judas, Scripture says:
"he . . . repented and brought back the thirty pieces of
silver to the chief priests and the elders, saying, 'I have
sinned in betraying innocent blood.' But they said, 'What
is that to us? See to it thyself.' And he flung the pieces of
silver into the temple, and withdrew; and went away and
hanged himself with a halter" (Mt. 27:3–5).

The story of Judas presents many reflections for each
of us and not the least ought to be that there is always
an awful difference when we look at sin before we do it
and after we commit it. Before we commit sin, the thing
to be gained seems so attractive and the transgression that
gains it seems so trifling and insignificant. But, oh, after
the sin is committed, the tables are turned and the thing
gained seems so contemptible and the transgression so great.
Thirty pieces of silver — pitch them into the temple and get
rid of them. The thing that we win is cursed in our grasp.
Take, for instance, something we know to be in violation of
the commandments of God, tempted to it by a momentary
indulgence of some mere animal impulse. How quickly it
dies in its satisfaction. It lasts but such a short time and
then we are left alone with the thought of the deed we
have done. Most of our earthly aims are like that and certainly all of our transgressions follow that formula. As the
silver Judas took to betray his God burned the palms of
his hands until he cast them from him like a viper that

stung his hands, so does the devil ever cheat the sinner of the substance for a shadow, and then robs him of that, or changes it into a frightful specter from which he would escape if he could.

Learn, too, that we may possess great privileges, make great profession of faith, fill high office, and still have no real piety. Again learn that there is a tremendous power in a guilty conscience to inflict punishment. Finally, learn that remorse alone is fruitless, but, if it leads to repentance and confession of sin born of a sorrow for having offended God, we can hope to follow Peter's example rather than that of Judas.

Would to God Judas had sought out Mary, the Mother of Mercy as John had done. How differently this tragic story might have ended! Her counsels, her prayers, and intercession would doubtlessly have won him a strengthening of hope. This very day, say a prayer to Our Lady of Hope asking her to fill your soul with the virtue of hope so essential to keep us from ever being swallowed up in the awful sea of despair.

Saturday After Passion Sunday

"NOW Jesus stood before the procurator; and the procurator asked him, saying, 'Art thou the King of the Jews?' Jesus said to him, 'Thou sayest it' " (Mt. 27:11).

St. Matthew's words "Now Jesus stood before the procurator" are certainly soul stirring words, for they point up the fact that He who shall judge the nations, Himself stands before Pontius Pilate to be judged. Pilate has won a terrible pre-eminence among the sons of Adam, for every child is taught to say that the Son of God "suffered under Pontius Pilate, was crucified, died, and was buried."

It would be an error to say that all those who had anything to do with the death of Christ were totally depraved. Certainly Pilate was not in this class. He was actually a reluctant agent. Pilate's sin was not so much that he failed to recognize the Messiasship of Christ, as rather that he condemned without evidence, that he acted against his own convictions, that he was influenced by the fear of man, that he had a sordid regard for place and power, which all led him to his condemnation of an innocent Man, and in so doing, he prostituted his office.

There is something of Pilate about all of us. Despite our avowals that we are followers of Christ — Christians — do we not all too frequently act against our convictions, and do we not fail to do the upright and noble thing because we fear the mob or because we have a servile love for human applause. Certainly we are other Pilates when we fear to say we are Catholics; when we are afraid to bow our head or tip our hat passing a church; when we are afraid to make the Sign of the Cross before our grace at meals; when we are afraid to refrain from eating between meals during Lent for fear of what others will think or say; when we are too timid to walk away from the person who insists on telling impure stories — these and a thousand other ways.

The sequel of Pilate's history is affecting and instructive. The thing he dreaded came to pass, for he lost the favor of the emperor and died a suicide.

There is another point in the story that calls for our studied attention. It was Pilate's question: "Art Thou the king of the Jews?"

Jesus did not look much like a king as He stood there, His hands bound, and a rope about His neck. Where was His power? Where was His throne, His crown, His scepter, His royal robes?

But to us today, how different does it all appear! Christ is throned, now, far above all principality and power, and might and dominion, as He sits at the right hand of His Father.

But what of Christ in the Holy Eucharist? He doesn't look much like a King in the tabernacles of our churches the world over. Before we place too much blame upon Pilate, let us look within our own souls and we shall doubtlessly discover that we, like Pilate, have somehow failed to realize the King of kings under the humble species of bread and wine.

Before we do another thing today, let us each make an act of faith in the Divine Presence of the King of kings in the Eucharist and beg that this faith be increased so that from today on, we shall never fail to visit Him daily — if even only for a moment. Beg, too, for the courage to follow always the dictates of our conscience, and never to compromise, no matter what the pressure, in matters of faith and morals.

Monday of Holy Week

THE whole sordid story of Christ's appearance before Pilate is one calculated to set the least of us to some deep thinking. It is frightening to ponder how close Pilate came to justification rather than to the depths of scorn earned by him for his weakness of character and the abuse of his authority.

Every possible way consistent with the preservation of his free will was used to save him. Divine Providence was at work to spare the governor from consummating his guilt. First, there was the silence of Christ. The Saviour who had cringed under the weight of our sins in the Garden of Gethsemani now stands erect, composed and silent — a demeanor bespeaking supernatural dignity. This affected Pilate so much that St. Matthew says "the procurator wondered exceedingly" (27:14). And even when Pilate had said the fateful words: "Take him yourselves and crucify him" (Jn. 19:6), yet another appeal was made to his conscience, for the Jews replied: "We have a Law, and according to that Law he must die, because he has made himself the Son of God" (Jn. 19:7). This open and pointed claim to supernatural, superhuman rank, did for a moment startle the weak Pilate, for Scripture says: "Now when Pilate heard this statement, he feared the more" (Jn. 19:8).

Certainly, the involuntary awe that first came over him as he faced the Innocent Christ must have settled over him now with greater force. No one, no matter how sinful and callous, could ever look upon the face of Christ and not sense His deity. Hence came forth the earnest question: "Where art thou from?" (Jn. 19:9.) There was never a moment during that dread scene of judgment when Pilate was far from doing the right and noble thing — never a moment when he was far from salvation. But alas, he suc- cumbed to criminal irresolution, he resisted impulses, he fled from the prods of conscience, he banished the warnings of his wife, and made instead, a weak concession to the fear of man. When Pilate condemned the Son of God without evidence and against his own convictions, he prostituted his high office.

Not until we stand before Christ in judgment will we ever know how often and with what great effort Christ has tried to save each one of us. We shall be confused and con- founded when we learn the amount of grace Christ showered upon us, often at the very moments when we were resisting the warnings of conscience, the pleading of parents, teachers, priests, and friends — bent upon doing our own will and seeking our own pleasures, albeit this involved the breaking of God's own laws.

Pilate had one golden opportunity, and he lost it. How much more culpable are we than Pilate, who, times without number, have rejected God's grace and resisted His agents, and been influenced to do evil through fear of what our fellow men would think or say?

Base and weak as Pilate was, he is in the record as having called Christ "A just Man." When you have thought long and well on what Christ has done for you, the graces with which He has showered you, I am sure you will be compelled to thank Him with all your soul because His mercy has outweighed His justice in your regard.

Tuesday of Holy Week

IT IS strange how often a person who is too weak of character to do what he knows to be right, will rack his brains for something to excuse him from doing his duty and thus will seize upon the first thing which comes to mind to relieve him of his dilemma. So it was with Pilate. He knew after he had questioned our Lord that He was guiltless, and that he should release Him. Then the thought struck him that perhaps if he offered to follow an ancient custom of releasing a prisoner on the eve of the great Jewish feast of Passover that he could manage, somehow, to have them choose Christ as against a murderer, and thus he would be rid of the problem. So he mentioned the custom to the Jews and as the alternative to Christ, he chose Barabbas — a robber, a rioter, "one who in the riot had committed murder" (Mk. 15:7).

Pilate said: " 'Which of the two do you wish that I release to you?' And they said 'Barabbas.' Pilate said to them: 'What then am I to do with Jesus who is called Christ?' They all said, 'Let him be crucified' " (Mt. 27:21, 22).

Never in the annals of human history has there been a greater example of the criminal evasion of personal responsibility. Here was Pilate, who in his heart knew that

Christ was innocent of any crime, and had said so in public, but now, in fact says to the mob, "you pick the victim and I'll sentence him whether he is guilty or not." Many of us today, who decry the weakness of Pilate, get much the same way on many occasions. We often allow others to determine our duty. Have we not all at times said something like this: "But every one does it"; or "Everyone else in the office tells off-color stories"; or "If my wife would be more religious, I'd be religious too"; or "If my husband didn't drink, I wouldn't drink," and so on.

Let us beg of God the grace to do what we know to be right and just, and for the grace to manfully withstand those who would even suggest our making concessions to evil because of our fear of man.

The second point of this consideration is equally important. Pilate poses one of the most striking questions formulated when he asked: "What then am I to do with Jesus who is called the Christ?" — a question Pilate and all of us are compelled to answer in the end. Jesus stands before each of us, as He stood before Pilate, demanding reception or rejection. The question may be postponed, but we cannot get it off our hands. Every soul must stand in judgment on Christ and give a decision.

Jesus stands before each of us today, meek and lowly, asking to be received; but the scene will soon be changed for those who reject Him. They will be hurried away to judgment in eternity, and the Judge before whose bar we shall find ourselves will be the same One who stood so long, so patient and loving, waiting to serve us.

Resolve to make a thorough examination of conscience daily on how you fulfill the duties of your state in life and to what extent you permit others to determine your duty. Ask yourself, too, this burning question: "What have I done today with Christ?" The answer God expects us to give is: "I have loved Him; I have obeyed Him in all things; I have served Him faithfully."

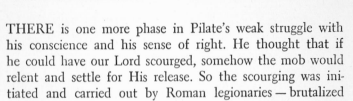

Wednesday of Holy Week

THERE is one more phase in Pilate's weak struggle with his conscience and his sense of right. He thought that if he could have our Lord scourged, somehow the mob would relent and settle for His release. So the scourging was initiated and carried out by Roman legionaries — brutalized instruments of a race noted for its absence of all tenderness.

St. John must have wept as he wrote these words: "Pilate, then, took Jesus and had him scourged" (Jn. 19:1), but St. Matthew was more reportorial, for he wrote: "Then the soldiers of the procurator took Jesus into the praetorium, and gathered together about him the whole cohort. And they stripped him and put on him a scarlet cloak; and plaiting a crown of thorns, they put it upon his head, and a reed into his right hand; and bending the knee before him they mocked him, saying, 'Hail, King of the Jews!' And they spat on him, and took the reed and kept striking him on the head" (Mt. 27:27–30).

The Romans used various kinds of scourges. There was the stick (*fustis*), the rod (*virga*), and the whip (*lorum*) which was of leather-platted thongs and into the plats were woven iron spikes (*scorpio*) or knuckle bones of animals. Tradition has it that the latter was used by the soldiers to scourge Christ.

Behold your Saviour bound to a low pillar with the six scourgers standing on a raised platform beside and above Him, and watch them, if you can, laying in those cruel lashes on the bent back of our Lord! Let us go to His side and gaze into the pure eyes of Christ as He suffers in the scourging and acknowledge that it was our sins — yours and mine — that caused Him to endure such agony, and promise Him that from this day on we shall never deliberately offend Him again.

There is another consideration I would have you ponder over in your mind. It concerns the reed placed in our Lord's hands during the crowning with thorns as a mock gesture of a king's scepter. Is it not worthy of note that the lowly reed should play such an important part in our Lord's life. He began His public life by going to Cana of Galilee, to begin as it were the reconstruction and redemption of mankind with a man and his wife — since it was a man and his wife who had opened the sluice gates of sin and flooded this world with woe. "Cana," you see, means "a place of reeds."

And now at the end of His public life the reed appears again and is placed in His hands in mockery of His royalty, and finally, it becomes an instrument of torture in itself — since the soldiers beat His thorn-crowned head with this same reed. I have always thought that the special sufferings inflicted on our Lord by the blows from the reed were in reparation for the mockery men and women make of marriage and the sins, such as divorce, abortion, desertion, and birth control committed by persons disdainful of God's laws. Married persons will beg for the grace to fulfill the duty of their state and the unmarried will beg special graces for those to whom God has entrusted such awful responsibilities.

Holy Thursday

"AND [they] led him away to crucify him. Now as they went out, they found a man of Cyrene named Simon; him they forced to take up his cross" (Mt. 27:31–32).

In the beginning there was no one to help our Lord carry His cross. Weak from the loss of sleep and from the cruel scourging and the crowning with thorns, and still more from the insults of His enemies and the desertion of His friends, which caused Him untold anguish, yet He was forced to carry the heavy cross. He did His very best until His nature gave way and thus He fell several times to the ground.

We must never lose sight of the fact that while our Lord had to carry the cross unaided, in reality it was not for Himself that He bore it, but for you and for me. He endured unbelievable pain and endured the shame and the insults, for all of us, that He might free us from the burden of the curse of sin.

When St. John the Baptist encountered Christ at the outset of His public life, he said to his followers: "Behold the Lamb of God, who takes away the sin of the world"

(Jn. 1:29). We must say the same words as we contemplate Christ carrying His cross, for that is exactly what He did. No, it was not only the wood of the cross that was so burdensome, rather it was the mountain of our sins. It was the loathsome weight of sin that caused our Saviour to falter and fall on the Way of the Cross.

Fearful that they would be deprived of the satisfaction of crucifying Him, the soldiers compelled a passer-by, Simon of Cyrene, to help our Lord. One can only imagine how much, at first, Simon must have resented this task, but picture Simon and Christ carrying the cross together — Jesus in front carrying the heavier part and Simon coming behind with its lighter end is both a sad and a consoling thought.

This is a true picture of every follower of Christ. We must all share the cross with Christ if we would reign with Him. Did our Lord not say: "He who does not take up his cross and follow me, is not worthy of me" (Mt. 10:38)?

There is great consolation in reversing the scene wherein Simon helps Jesus carry His cross and contemplating it in a new light — that of Christ helping Simon carry the cross. You see, once Simon was pressed into service by the soldiers, our Lord did not abandon him and leave him to struggle with the load alone. Indeed not. Christ, weak as He was, placed His bruised and torn shoulder under the heavier part.

Every cross we have to bear will find Christ's shoulder beneath it, and, indeed, beneath the heavy end of it. There is no cross we are unable to bear with Jesus helping us. No load He shares will ever crush us, for we have His infallible word: "Come to me, all you who labor and are burdened, and I will give you rest" (Mt. 11:28).

Make acts of contrition for your sins that added to the weight of the cross on the way to Calvary; thank Him for having taken away your sins; and thank Him for having always helped you carry your crosses thus far in life.

Christ refused the potion that His sufferings might not be lessened. But Christ gives us His body, blood, soul, and divinity as our food to strengthen us to bear our sufferings and to carry our crosses. In the Eucharist, the Stronger helps the weaker.

Good Friday

"AND they came to the place called Golgotha, that is, the Place of the Skull. And they gave him wine to drink mixed with gall; but when he had tasted it, he would not drink" (Mt. 27:34). "Then they crucified him" (Mk. 15:24).

The object behind the offering of the stupefying draught for those sentenced to undergo crucifixion was that it would produce a partial unconsciousness, so that the terrible agonies might not be so keenly felt. But it will be noted that our Lord would not accept anything that would lessen His sufferings. He did taste it so that the Scripture might be fulfilled, for David had said of the Messias, in prophecy: "And they gave me gall for my food; and in my thirst they gave me vinegar to drink" (Ps. 68:22). Scripture thus fulfilled, our Lord refused to do more than taste of it, since He did not seek to lessen in any way the bitterness of the cup which His Father had given Him to drink.

There is an important lesson for all of us in this incident in the Passion of our Lord and that lesson is that we are always more Christlike when we accept the crosses and trials of this life as they come to us, seeing in them golden opportunities for making reparation for our own sins and the sins of the world, and at the same time, seeing all such crosses as sent to us by God for our spiritual benefit. As Christians we are not bound to seek suffering, but when it comes in the path of duty, let us meet it calmly, resolutely, and fearlessly.

"Then they crucified him" (Mk. 15:24). To the devout Christian every item of information he can gain concerning that dread scene at Calvary is of the utmost value. The horrible act of crucifixion itself was foreign to the Jewish people, for it was of Roman origin, and the sufferings it caused signifies the extreme anguish to which human sensibility can go. It was long and lingering in its operation. Apart from the agony inflicted by the nailing of the hands and feet, even greater suffering was inflicted by the constrained posture on the cross. And there hung the Son of God, the Redeemer of the world, suspended between heaven and earth for three long and agony-filled hours until the full debt for your sins and mine was paid. What a terrible thing sin must be, that its expiation required such a sacrifice! The hearts of all who dwell on the picture of Christ dying on the cross must of necessity be stirred to beg for the grace to avoid ever committing a deliberate mortal sin again. How can we ever in the future be careless about sinning when we contemplate what our Lord suffered to save us from our sins? And what can we say of the wonderful love God must have for sinful man to cause Him to give His Son to endure such a death to save him!

Make time today to go, in spirit, to Calvary's hill and take your place beside the sinless Mary, the Virgin Mother of Christ, and beside the sinner Mary Magdalen. Your own selfish sinful heart will know what to say to Christ as He hangs on the cross. Tell Him of how you thank Him for what He has done for you and beg of Him the special grace to know the vileness and tragedy of sin.

The price has been paid. Christ died on the cross. But men, forgetting the awful ransom paid by our Lord, go right on sinning. Hear our Lord say to Mother Marie Saint-Cecile of Rome: "I understand human frailty. I forgive readily, I forget indelicacies as soon as the soul returns to Me, but that does not prevent My Heart from feeling the wound."

Promise our Lord today that never again will you wound His Sacred Heart by sin. Make the slogan of St. Dominic Savio your motto: "Death rather than mortal sin."